MY LIFE IN ART

SCHLOSS ORT. GMUNDEN, AUSTRIA
Gouache, 1955.   22½″ x 30″

MY Life
in
ArT
Bemelmans

ANDRE DEUTSCH: LONDON

FIRST PUBLISHED 1958 BY
ANDRE DEUTSCH LIMITED
12–14 CARLISLE STREET SOHO SQUARE
LONDON W I
© LUDWIG BEMELMANS 1954, 1958
PRINTED IN GREAT BRITAIN BY
D. R. HILLMAN AND SONS LTD
FROME SOMERSET

MY LIFE IN ART

I.

SWAN COUNTRY

As it is now, so it was then, only more so—a setting like the scenery for a Viennese operetta. A place in which, a plot in which nothing violent would happen. The décor was in pastel colors, gay and simple and immediately understood. In it people walked about in lovely costumes.

There was music everywhere. Men in uniforms, women who were elegant. Peasant women in beautifully embroidered silks. The emperor had a villa close by and a joke was told about Francis Joseph, who was a serious man.

He had invited the Danny Kaye of those days, a comedian named Giradi, to cheer him up. They sat opposite each other and there was silence and then the emperor said: "Why don't you say something funny?"

Giradi replied: "What could you say that's funny when you lunch with the emperor?"

There was no radio, no television, nothing but music and conversation, and life was comfortable. Like the pages of a children's book, the days were turned and looked at, and the most important objects in this book were the sun, the moon and the stars; people, flowers and trees. Large trees, whose leaves throbbed with color and who reached up to the sky—black tree trunks, sometimes brownish black and shining in the rain, with

the leaves smelling—young in spring, and yellow in the autumn, when each leaf in the light of afternoon was like a lamp lit up. Pink and violet clouds, and flowers very clear and close, for when one is small one can put one's face to them easily and breathe in their fragrance, and look at them close. Does one ever see things clearer than as a child? The sky is blue, the gardener's apron is greener than spinach. The eyes of Gazelle are large and brown and kind.

A whistle is heard; a ship approaches. Suddenly it is close and big as a house, alive and floating, snow white and gold among the lavished wealth of color of garden, field and mountains. The ship's name is *Elisabet*. She turns and in a dead slowdown comes to the dock. The reflection wobbles for a while in the broad waves the ship made when the arrested paddlewheel dragged along. Now the captain waves, and I wave back, and then after a little while the captain pulls a cord. One sees this and a puff of white steam flowing upward, and then the sound of the steamer whistle is heard again. The steamer ripples the water, the floating deck makes a gurgling sound. The "phlop, phlop, phlop" of the paddlewheels has stopped.

When the ship approaches, the swans go this way and that on the water, and when they hear its whistle they leave to make room for the *Elisabet*, and one of them, our swan, stretches, rises out of the water, beats his wings, and then awkwardly runs on the soles of his feet with much splashing, half running, half flying on the water. He finally takes off, with labored flight; he stretches his neck, making a straight long line; he sails overhead and then comes down; he lands with a swishing beat of wings, with his webbed feet stretched out in front of him—bracing himself against the water. He

has his wings outstretched still and then folds them, and from a high, standing position he becomes suddenly the beautiful swan in the lake. He comes to our dock and climbs out. He is the most enterprising of the swans.

We eat in summer in what was once a hothouse and is now a dining room. My Papa is an impatient perfectionist, which makes life difficult for him. He has to have everything beautiful at once, and because it takes all summer for the grapes to ripen he has placed glass grapes among the foliage, and put electric lights in them. They hang among the thick foliage in what is called the *vignoble*, for we speak only French in this garden. The vines are dark green at the ceiling and light green along the sides. The swan waits to be fed, making sounds of impatience with his beak, as if he were a goose, sometimes even hissing when he has to wait too long.

The little city of Gmunden, on the Traunsee, in the Austrian province of Salzkammergut, is very cosmopolitan. The Duke of Cumberland has a vast estate there. The Queen of Greece was born there, and last year, when I went back to paint Schloss Ort, there was a car ahead of me with number 21 on a blue license plate, and it was she, who had come back to look at the beautiful lake and the scenes of childhood.

My father was a Belgian and a painter who had inherited property in Gmunden. Besides the mansion which, with its trees and park, stood surrounded by water, he owned a hotel called "The Golden Ship."

Its clientele was remarkable for variety and character. There came every year a Russian grand duke who occupied two floors. There were Parisians, Americans, Germans, Greeks—every nationality. I saw Papa rarely, and my mother I don't remember at all in those days. I lived with my governess in the garden on the lake. She was young and French. I could not say "Mademoiselle" then, and addressed her as "Gazelle."

Papa, when he came to the place where I lived with Mademoiselle, was always busy arranging *plaisanteries*. He built me a complete little carpenter shop where I could work and paint alone and in which he never, as normal fathers would, puttered himself. He had his own workshop where he busied himself with modeling in clay, making frames, designing machinery and inventing. He was never without a project. He created the first Pedalo, a water-going bicycle, which he tried out on the lake. It was elaborate and in the shape of a swan. He had a very beautiful, small motorcar made for me and he presented me with these toys very formally and with an air of apology that made it difficult for me to thank him, or show my enthusiasm in full. I have inherited this and am very embarrassed when anyone thanks me for anything.

Papa sometimes came and sketched Gazelle wearing a helmet or a cuirass. He was fond of armor and collected it. He played the guitar and had a very good voice. The song he liked most to sing was "Ouvre tes yeux bleus, ma mignonne." He dressed unlike other people, in velvet jackets, corduroy suits, large black hats, and flowing ties. He wore a mustache and a beard. He had very small feet, a whipping walk and small, nervous hands.

Papa sometimes would paint in the garden. He brought a small easel, a large palette and put on a blue smock. But he never painted me; he always looked at me with the curiosity of a stranger meeting someone for the first time. I bowed to him, he bowed to me.

I was presented to him, always carefully washed and dressed. He approved to the extent that he decided to make use of me as an angel during Christmas when I was four years old. Papa gave a Christmas party for the employees of the hotel and for the fishermen, boatmen and peasants. A large table was in the center of the ballroom of the hotel, with gifts for the children. My golden curls were especially curled and brushed and they had made white wings for me and attached them to my shoulders. Overhead on the ceiling was a pulley, and a hook was attached to some white satin which had been wrapped around my middle, and I was pulled upward on a rope and suspended above the Christmas tree. I disappointed him badly, for the smell of burning wax candles, the pipe smoke, the heat and the fear of falling made me ill. I was taken down and abruptly dismissed. I cried, and Gazelle cried—and we went back to the security of our little park.

Papa surrounded himself with friends who, like himself, were determined to be outstandingly different from the provincial citizenry and the staid aristocrats who lived in Gmunden. Their worries were about the next day's happiness, which they made

like the baker his rolls, and always while whistling, singing or reeling in their fish. They found caves to illuminate at night and gave parties in them. They covered wooden floats with flowers and sailed them on the lake. They sent off rockets that awoke the town and exploded high in the sky and filled the night with a rain of phosphorescent stars that were all reflected in the lake. They gave concerts, sang operas and acted in their own plays, and Papa was the president of a gay society which was called "Schlar-affia."

The hotel existed merely to cater to these celebrations. The maître d'hôtel, Monsieur Zobal, a very distinguished-looking, quiet, small man, who invariably wore snow-white linen and tailcoat, was busy blowing up balloons, helping Papa gild plaster statues, setting off fireworks and stringing up lampions.

Above all I admired his skill with napkins. After deft and precise folding of the snow-white linen, he turned the napkins with a last twist into the shapes of fans, ships, plants and swans. He also chiseled swans and castles out of blocks of ice. Whenever there was something especially good for dessert over in the hotel, Monsieur Zobal saved some of it for us and brought it across the next day.

In the hothouse where we ate the meals were gay. We sat facing the lake; there were Papa's dogs who came and the swan. There was conversation and, in two carafes, red and white wine. Gazelle drank out of a glass on a thin stem; I had a little golden mug with my name written on it. Monsieur Zobal brought gifts and the chef sometimes came himself. The swan was sometimes rough in his affection for me and once knocked me off balance and into the lake. Gazelle jumped in and saved me.

We left the house at nine on our daily walk, hand in hand, along the promenade. I was always neatly dressed, my curls combed, my shoelaces properly tied and always with white gloves. I was her little blue fish, her little treasure, her small green duckling, her dear sweet cabbage, her amour.

14

Summer, winter, autumn, spring—there was every day a long promenade with
Gazelle, and we always came to a place with thistly bushes, where quinces grew, and

then to a garden and a field, rose colored with the blossoms of heather, and after that to a small inn, where cakes and chocolate were served.

All is still there—quinces, heather, the small inn, all unchanged. The daughter now runs the inn but she has the same smile, the same voice, the same ease and air of comfort and of peace that her mother had.

This intimate life in the small park and the old house on the lake—being bathed, dressed, fed, cared for—was only clouded by such tragedies as having toenails cut or getting soap into my eyes, when the big, clear tears of childhood rolled down my cheeks.

The other person who cried frequently was God. The God of that time and garden in Gmunden was "Le Bon Dieu" who worried only about making this life beautiful, and from whom all good things came. He was a beautiful old grandfather, and when it rained it was because people were bad; He had to cry and the tears ran over His cheeks and down His beard and over the lake. Mademoiselle said that the Bon Dieu was everywhere in every flower, animal and cloud. And therefore one did not need to go to church.

I never was visited by other children. These long years of childhood were spent in the seclusion of the park and the vast house alone with Gazelle.

Monsieur Zobal came over to supervise the cooking, which was French. Papa came also when he needed the hothouse to celebrate in or to rehearse musicians, or when he tied his sailboat to the dock.

One time, when I was six, he wanted to take me on a drive around the country.

Among the few German words I knew was *Pferd*, which means horse; the coachman's name was Ferdinand, and because he had to do with horses I called him Pferdinand.

The coach, like everything Papa had, was an extraordinary vehicle, a shiny black landau, the body suspended on heavy straps of red Russian leather with gilt buckles. Pferdinand in top hat and livery and a bear rug over his legs waited. Two white Borzoi dogs also waited to run after us.

B

This was to be a family outing and Mama came and sat down in the carriage. I was handed over, with my golden curls squeezed down by a hat held in place with a stinging rubber band. Whenever I was taken from the side and hand of Gazelle, there were tears. I sat and cried as we waited. At last Papa came, looked at me seated in the coach and, lifting his hat, he said to Mama that he was sorry but he couldn't come, because it would bore him. "I'll talk to him, later—when he understands—when he is seventeen," he said, and turned on his heel. As on that Christmas night when I had been an angel, I was happy again to be handed back to Gazelle, who cried also, and then Le Bon Dieu started to cry—it rained. It rained almost every day in Gmunden—rain that sounded like the water of a shower falling full force on bathwater in the tub. It rained especially when one thought that it would be a lovely day, and when there was a patch of pale blue sky overhead in the morning.

It still rained when I was there last year. I painted the castle in rain. On this voyage I became aware that my palette is still of that landscape in rain.

The colors of houses and landscapes mostly in rain sank into my eyes in early childhood. This time, spent in a restricted place and in solitude, impressed on me the objects in nature which I still see in the shape and colors in which they were.

There was often fog on the lake. The fog was green, blue, violet, gray; it floated into the garden like gauze. It stood sometimes in shapes under trees, then disappeared as it had come. It determined the coloration of water, of the swans, of the eyes of Gazelle and of her hair. And sometimes it was like an immense white shroud, covering all. When the wind tore into it, it moved, and there suddenly appeared again the lake, the *Elisabet*, a swan, the bridge. On my recent visit the old steamer was still paddling "Phlop, phlop, phlop" around the lake.

The seasons passed slowly in my childhood. There were the many phases of spring, with snow melting and running off the roofs, and icicles falling, and the birds drinking in the puddles made by the dripping water, and the sun reflecting in them. One of the many miracles I beheld then was the reflection of the sun in every puddle, even the smallest and dirtiest ones. My favorite season was autumn, the rich autumn of russet and of all the dark reds and umber, the yellow autumn when all the chestnut trees were lit up with sun, and another phase when the leaves had fallen and the ground was a tapestry of ochre leaves with the trunks of trees turned several shades darker. I remember the smells of autumn, of ripening fruit along the espalier trees, especially of apricots, which were harvested and taken to the chef. He made from them my favorite dessert— dumplings of light dough with an apricot inside and bread crumbs and sugar outside. This dessert is called *Marillenknoedel*—and I was able to eat a dozen of them at one sitting.

Then the last stage of autumn, the park cleared of the ochre leaves, the promenades swept, the trees now bare and the leaves sunk down to the bottom of the lake, shining upward and gilding the water. And, finally, the *Elisabet* was put to bed for

CMUNDEN

the winter on the other side of the lake, tied to a dock next to a tavern. And one day she was covered and went to sleep under a coverlet of snow.

Long hours now were spent indoors with the collection of postal cards of Paris, the Album of Paris, the children's stories of France, the songs written for French children.

And then one autumn the leaves in the park were not raked, the swan stood there forlorn and it was all over—all had come to an end. Papa was gone and so was my governess, and I wished so much that he had run away with Mama and left me Gazelle.

Every child in his youngest years is a good artist, mostly of the abstract and expressionist school of painting. At about the age of twelve, this universal endowment is withdrawn. Children then become conscious of objects.

Art is mostly emotion and emotion fades away when purposeful thinking takes the upper hand.

This happened to me. There came many, many years in which I had the desire to paint, but I created only pictures with a purpose. I came to America, illustrated the books and stories I wrote. I painted theatrical scenery. I did pictures and covers for magazines. My work was mostly in black and white, water color and gouache.

I began really to paint in the summer of 1953 in Campobello and around there, where the clear landscapes and fresh, simple colors were easy to my brush. I was always afraid of nature; that is, the business of putting up an easel and unpacking colors and painting this tree, landscape, person or object had something of invading privacy about it. I made sketches and took them home, but then found that the immediacy of the scene in front of one's eyes was lost. I started to hide away in places and paint, and then found that there were things one cannot render in black and white, in line, with pencil, or pen and ink, water color or gouache, and that they had to be painted in oil. Or I should say, perhaps, that I could not render them in these media to conform with the image that was in my eye, or what I wanted the picture to be. This is an agonizing period for an artist; one might as well have stumps for arms—it is impossible to reach for the brush and to paint. There is the image, and beyond reach.

There are words to describe this better, but my point is simple. You are dry inside with a kind of thirst and hunger until you accomplish that which you must do. I suppose it is one of the manifestations of nature, the same command that drives a homing pigeon to its destiny, causes a new shape and color of leaf to grow or a new idea to form itself in the head of a scientist or thinker.

I am not a practical person, not logical and not a thinker. I can't learn anything except by my senses and I am impeded by a self-indulgent strain for pleasure and comfort. The matter of painting in oil I knew would give me many miserable hours. I had avoided the issue for years and argued with myself that there was no real reason why I should paint in oil. But the inner voice of the bothersome self persisted and there was regularly this kick of conscience so that I finally pulled myself together and, marshaling what discipline I had, dragged myself over the rotten road.

When such rare manifestation of character on my part occurs, then with some painful delay, never at once, whatever force directs my life eventually comes to my aid. Always in curious places, when I least expect it and this time really at the last moment.

And so in this matter. I took little joy in buying the palette, the heavy tubes of oil color. There came a period of evasion, waste of time and money, and finally in the disastrous circumstances described in the next chapter, there came the needed aid. It started with the search for a studio. I always begin things with as much confusion and elaborate setting-up of scenery as possible.

2.

PARIS

In Paris I lived in a penthouse, in a house that belonged once to the chef of Louis XIV. It was the color of cold salmon and stood on the left bank facing the Seine, on the Quai des Grands-Augustins, at the corner where the Rue Gît-le-Coeur meets the quai. It had a two-person elevator, a statue by Rodin in the entrance hall, and the top floors were furnished like a country house in Westchester. It belonged to an American lady, Miss Alice de la Mar, who rented it to me.

From its roof terrace you could see all that is most beautiful in Paris: the sweeping pano-
rama of the city, the Cathedral of Notre Dame, Montmartre, the Seine, and even the
Eiffel Tower. My dog, a bouvier des Flandres, was with me.

At the time, I was working on an article on the Paris underworld for *Holiday*
magazine. I spent a good part of the nights in the rough quarters around the Place Pig-
alle and La Chapelle. I found out what I wanted about crime and the police, for that
is easy enough, both sets of actors in this drama being eager to explain why they are on
this or that side of the heavy doors. A group of Parisians that are more difficult to know
and live in the shadows are the antisocial people who are called *clochards*. A clochard is
usually mistaken by non-Parisians for a beggar. He is however intensely respectable,
but wants to have nothing to do with life as it is lived by his fellow citizens in stations
below or above him. He despises the beggar, the criminal, the police, the bourgeoisie
high and low, the aristocracy, the civil servant, the religious, the good and righteous,
conservative and radical and all other political parties, with equal vehemence. He lives a
hard life, sleeping under bridges, collecting cigar or cigarette butts, which are sold at a
special market. He also collects old paper, bottles and shoes, string, rags and other waste
materials. In contrast to the people who are called *chiffoniers* and who do this regularly
in day-to-day labor, he works only when he must have a meal or a bottle of the very
cheapest wine.

There are married clochards and also a few women clochards. In the summer,
they arrange themselves, leaning against trees along the Seine; in cold weather, they dis-
appear into cellars or wander south. From one of the windows of the apartment in the
house at Number 1 Rue Gît-le-Coeur, I observed a clochard who lived under the Pont-
Neuf. I watched him for weeks. He had a mattress on which he slept under the arch of
the bridge that rests on the Left Bank. For his collection, he used an old baby carriage,

and at night this baby carriage was the place where his small fox terrier slept. He was a clochard who shaved every day—most of them wear beards. After rising, he rolled up his mattress and tied it with a string; then he stuck into it the sack that covered the dog. He had an empty can, on a string, which he let down into the Seine and brought up filled. He heated the water on some sticks, then put a broken mirror on a small ledge formed by the stonework of the bridge and there he shaved. He had a box attached to the back of the baby carriage with dry pieces of bread and some wine in it—that was his breakfast. The preparation of his toilette, the eating of breakfast, the stowing away of the gear, all done in his own good time, took about two hours and were followed by playing with his dog, stretching, and, on bright days, by careful washing of his shirt, which he dried while the sun shone on his back.

Sometimes he sat in the sun and watched the patient fishermen, who never seem to catch anything. Or else he admired the women on the barges which are tied along that stretch of the quais. Not their beauty, for they are all hard-looking laboring women. What he admired with reserve was their forever cleaning the already shining boats, watering plants, painting, hanging up laundry, carrying things home from market. He never seemed bored.

Occasionally he was visited by a little girl, pale-faced and thin. She accompanied him on his walks when the weather was nice and played with the dog. Clochards don't like to be asked personal questions and I never found out who the little girl was.

Several days a week at about eleven in the forenoon, he decided to go and do that minimum of work that guaranteed his freedom. He slipped on a coat and a slouch hat with holes in it and, with the dog dancing ahead of him, in his stilted fox terrier way, the clochard pushed the baby carriage up to the Quai des Grands-Augustins and disappeared into the street next to La Pérouse. The kitchen window of this restaurant is at street

29

level and open except on the coldest days. The kitchen was his first stop. He inhaled the warm vapors of cooking and sometimes even stopped to inspect the luxurious garbage of this establishment.

The clochard then took various routes, his eyes mostly on the ground. He passed the markets, where he found overripe bananas, discarded greens, pieces of potatoes, and arrived eventually at a bistro to rest, to listen to gossip, to read the paper and to drink one small glass of a cheap, drinkable red wine.

I observed him daily at his bridge with my binoculars, and I followed him at a distance to his bistro. I was too busy with crime and the police to stay always on his track. But during the day, around noon, I used to give my dog a run at the quai near the bridge below. I saw the mattress there every day, and when he was not there got into the habit of sticking a half pack of American cigarettes, some once-used razor blades, a piece of soap, and some other small clochard's gift into the mattress. Then I watched him in the morning, trying out the new blade or smelling the soap. It was like befriending a squirrel in a park, a wildlife project.

Eventually, an overcoat was beyond its last dry cleaning; it was a warm, heavy dark blue coat become shiny. I took it down one autumn day, when it was getting cold, and left it toward evening, before his habitual hour of return.

I was amused by seeing my coat walking over the bridge the next day, topped by a hat I had given him. This was a bowler, a new hat, which made my face even rounder than it already is. He seemed to enjoy these acquisitions and nothing happened until a little man who sold gasoline along the Quai des Grands-Augustins told the clochard that the coat and hat he wore came from the fifth floor of Number 1 Rue Gît-le-Coeur.

He appeared there one day and acknowledged the receipt of the coat, the hat and the smaller gifts without exactly thanking me for them. He offered instead to do something for me in return.

"I have a vast store of information about this part of the city, it is my quartier. I know every house around here and across on the Island. If you are interested in anything, present or past, ask me. I know the quartier inside out; I was born a few houses from here."

He told me that he had been what is called a respectable citizen at one time, in so-called good circumstances, a teacher of history in a lycée for young ladies of good family.

"Oh, not what you think happened—God forbid! It was just that I was in steady conflict with the director. The maniacal principal of this institute almost drove me to suicide. I had to leave or I would have killed him."

One day he had decided that he was unhappy and had had enough and that he could no longer bear the burden of his bourgeois existence. He lived on the top floor of an apartment house on the Boulevard St. Michel. He opened the window and let out a bird he had kept in a cage, a finch. Then he threw the cage out of the window and all the papers of his pupils which he was correcting; they fluttered away like happy little sails, this way and that.

"I had the most beautiful sensation watching them. Finally I threw out all the rest of my possessions. Below in the street a vast throng formed as the things came down, photograph albums, shoe trees, lamp shades, bills, letters, all things that complicate life, and the old typewriter. I looked down first, for I did not want to give cause for trouble or hurt anyone. I only wanted to get rid of my personal belongings, of my tiresome identity.

"The eyes of the people below were alight with envy at this performance and some took the things and carried them away. Finally the police came, but there was nothing except a little explaining to do at the commissariat, and I was free—and so I shall stay. But what can I do for you?"

I said that I, too, envied him but that I had not yet reached his state of independence and still chose to remain imprisoned within my bourgeois walls.

"One must respect the ideas of others," he said simply. "I am not a fanatic. I do not try to change anything in this world, except I did change my own life, and for the better. But tell me, what is there I can do for you?"

I told him that like him and everyone else I had a desire to change my environment. My problem was that I, all my life, had passionately wanted to paint, and never found the right place and the time. Now I had the time. At long last I wanted to give myself to painting alone and was looking for a place in which to live and work.

I wanted to own an old house—like the one I lived in—because where I resided was a place merely rented to me by a good friend. I was in need of a place, facing north, in which I could have my studio and do nothing but paint.

"It may take time. I will try and find an old house for you," he said simply and, putting on my hat, he left.

I saw him occasionally in the years that followed, and one day in the spring of 1953 he said that he had found the house, and that I was to come right along.

"When we get there, walk past it, but don't go in yourself, for that would raise the price; I shall arrange everything. I have a friend who is an advocate, a decent one who defends prostitutes and the unfortunates of the underworld. I have told him of you and he will attend to the business part of the transaction. For a while you will not be able to live in the house as it is; it has no water, no electricity, no gas, no plumbing, but it is exactly what you are looking for."

We walked to the front of Notre Dame, turned left, walked down to the Seine, turned right, came to a blue-painted laundry, turned right again, and there it was.

At Number 4 Rue de la Colombe. It was precisely what I had been looking for —a lovely house, half palace, half ruin, an old house covered partly with vine. It had a bistro on the ground floor frequented by clochards and a small garden in front in which people sat. The professor said:

"If you look over the door, you will see the ancient name of this street cut into a stone. It was called at one time 'Rue d'Enfer'—the street of hell—and if ever you want to get rid of the clochards, just let someone clean up the bistro, or paint a wall; they will flee as if from a blinding flash. Then you can do with the place as you wish."

We sat down in the garden and he said: " 'This is the head, the heart, and the marrow of Paris,' as Gui de Bazoches wrote in the twelfth century of the Ile de la Cité. It was also compared to the prow of a ship that got stuck in the Seine. It is the most medieval part of Paris and retains its original aspect, especially on the corner where this old house faces its small private square. It was built in 1225 and later became the hôtel particulier of the mistress of François Premier, 'La belle Ferronnière.' In the adjoining street lived Héloïse and Abélard. The house became a tavern later and the hangout of François Villon. It was built in part from boulders which formed the ramparts of Lutetia, as Paris was then known when it consisted only of this island. The old house became a hotel eventually and was known as the Hôtel St.-Julien-le-Pauvre, named after a saint whose church stands across the Seine on the Left Bank."

With the help of the underworld advocate, I bought the house. I found a quaint architect with a beard and a pipe, which was mostly cold. He had a great feeling for what I had in mind.

"Touching—touching," he said between sucks on his cold pipe. "One would not expect such understanding from an American. Very touching."

Of the old house, the shell was to be left undisturbed, but the inside completely rebuilt. The bistro would remain as it was, above this would be my apartment, above this I would break through a floor and make a duplex studio overlooking the Seine. I wanted to install steam heat, an elevator, move the kitchen to the basement and, on the roof, build a garden and a hothouse. The architect made plans, and said that it would be difficult, but that he had great friends among the officials on whose good will one was dependent. He lit his pipe and looked at me through his sharp glasses. "Besides, for a foreigner, distinguished as you are, monsieur, and a great ami de la France exceptions will most certainly be made." He bowed. I looked at my house and saw it as it would be, filled with music, gaiety and life, twenty-four hours a day.

Paris is a village. Soon everybody knew about the Colombe and people came every day to inspect the house. They looked at me with envy and wives said to their husbands: "Why don't you ever think of anything like this?" or they said to me: "How clever of you, what a brilliant idea, how did you ever find this wonderful house? And to think of having one's own bistro and sidewalk café in Paris—and to get your liquor and wine wholesale and all your meals free—open day and night—no entertainment worries, five for dinner or fifty—and no servant problems. Do you know of any other such place for sale?" To this I could shake my head wisely and say "No," and all the people who stood around, neighbors, clochards and workingmen, also shook their heads, and murmured that this kind of thing happened only once. Several offers were made then to buy the house, and I could have sold it at great profit.

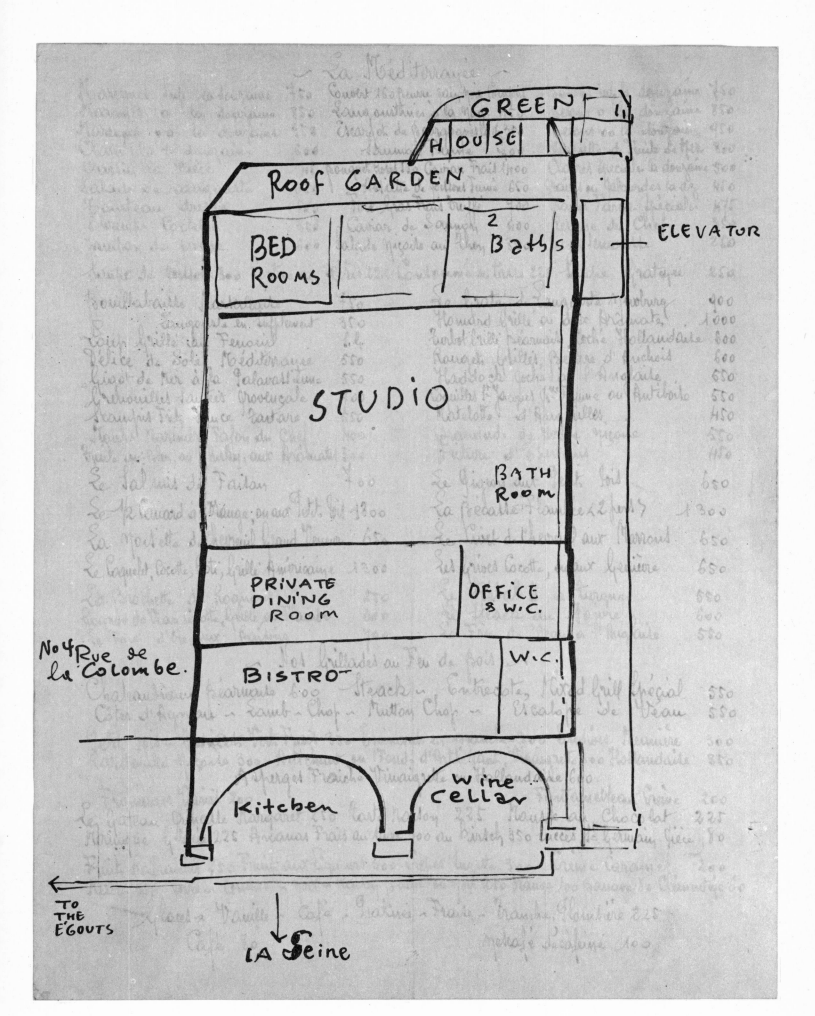

My friend Jean is the owner of the restaurant La Méditerranée. Sitting at my usual table there, every night, on the back of menus I had drawn and revised the plans for the old house and finally arrived at what it eventually would be like. Jean came to the Colombe every day; he would say, "It always takes an outsider to find a good thing like this. You know, whenever I am worried, in unhappy times, I come down here to get away. I promenade up and down, in these streets and on this little square. Oh, how often have I sat here—in this lovely green tunnel quietly drinking a petite coupe of the wine, which isn't bad at all. How stupid of me! I must have passed here a thousand times; I saw it—why didn't I buy it! However, I am glad it's yours now." He shook my hand and wished me luck. "Not that you need it, a house like this, a palace. You will live like a prince. And how quiet it is, no traffic, only the bells of Notre Dame. What poetry in this corner, what beauty, and how practical! You even have a private place to park your car—and the little garden covered with vine. I have a friend who is the head gardener at the Luxembourg; I will bring him, and he will look at the vine and have it properly taken care of." He started off on his long legs and then came back again.

"Would you consider selling me a half interest in the bistro? We'll get rid of the clochards, we'll make a terrace here, I will relieve you of all the worry. I am sure, mark my words, this will be a gold mine."

I like Jean very much, but I did not want a gold mine, I merely wanted to have this house as it was, and its spell unbroken, and that could not be done, with Jean. He is a good restaurateur, but he loves business and worships money. I go to his restaurant sometimes, and he sits there and looks as if he were about to cry. I ask him why and he says: "Look at the empty tables." Then a half hour after when the place is filled, he still looks sad, and I ask him: "What's wrong now?" and he says, "Yes yes, it's full now, but remember how it looked half an hour ago!"

So I told him. "No, thank you, but stay my friend and help me."

"Ah, yes," he said. "I have been thinking of the opening. Let me do the opening. I will take care of everything; we shall invite the most important people in Paris and have the best wines, a memorable menu—une fête, a celebration. Music, flowers, it will be wonderful."

I said that perhaps we could ask everyone to dress in the costumes of the period. People could come as François Premier, as La belle Ferronnière, as Héloïse and Abélard, as Quasimodo and Esmeralda. There was a role for everyone.

"We must get busy with the invitations," said Jean. "This will be the Paris party of the year." We sat down under the vine with the architect. The date was set for the opening. Plenty of time for engraved invitations—almost a year. And more people came, and stood about and said: "How wonderful," and some said: "How is it that such things only happen to him?" And Jean observed: "It's very simple—because he makes them happen! That's how anything happens in this world."

The architect came one morning, sat down in the garden, took the pipe out of his mouth and announced that we had to make the first démarche to the authorities, to obtain a permit. He interrupted himself, saying that he would explain on the way to the commissariat—there were some papers to fill out, and did I have my birth certificate with me?

I said: "No, I'm not even sure when I was born. It says in my passport April 27, 1898, but my mother said it was at 3 A.M. the last day of April."

"But has this uncertainty never troubled you?" asked the architect.

"No, on the contrary," I said.

"That will make it complicated as far as the authorities go," he said sucking in air. He then departed to inquire what to do.

Jean of the Méditerranée came, as he did every day on his way back from market. "Is there anything I can do for you?" he asked as he always did.

I told him that it was time to think of a staff. Did he know of any nice people to work for the Colombe?

"I have exactly the person for you. She is sent from heaven. She is the equivalent of the entire staff of a house. She will cook, clean, inside, outside, do everything. You won't need anyone else. She will save you her salary in repairs alone." He referred to her as *la mère machine*. This extraordinary person presented herself on the afternoon of that same day. She was as old as the stone of the house, a little woman, dressed in black, a working monster with hands and a face as if cut from tree root. She attached herself to the building immediately and knocked about in cellar, in attic and on the stairs. Her head was in the position of the beak of a pitcher from which one pours water, and by stiffness of joint confined to one movement, to the left or right, as are the heads of puppets. My dog Bosie shied from her at first sight and always squeezed past her on the stairs to avoid touch or caress. Her voice rasped; her eyes blinked like those of an owl. She fitted well into the street of hell. She held things as in a vise and she was never seated; she never leaned on anything or was in repose. With a broom she would start to clear the small garden and then to inspect the doors for security. On the door that led from the street into the dining room was an ancient lock, from which the key was missing. The place had been closed every night by putting in front of it a weighty iron grille and keeping this in place with a heavy chain. I did away with the grille and the chain and told la mère machine to go and get a locksmith and have a key made for the door. She twisted her head so that she could give me a quick glance. "You will never get anywhere if for every little thing you call in plumbers, electricians, mechanics, who are all robbers, crooks and wasters of time," she croaked. "I will take off this lock and find a key. No use throwing away money!"

There was then near the Bastille, spread over the length of the sidewalks there, a junk and old iron market, an annual affair called La Foire à la Féraille.

La mère machine took the lock off the door and, with it in her hands, tried several hundred keys, rusty and of all kinds of design; going from one heap of old iron to the other, after a search that took hours, she finally found a key that fitted this lock. This gave her immense satisfaction.

The salary of la mère machine was fifty dollars a month. Like the clochard she had a mattress; she had it in the house, I don't know where she put it at night to sleep on. She marketed and, like the clochard, looked under the stands for vegetables that had dropped, or been discarded, and put these into her shopping net along with the things she bought, after smelling, feeling and berating the article in question, often tasting it. There were small tangerines called *Clémentines,* overripe and discolored. Of these la mère machine bought half a dozen, at about one cent apiece, but not before one had been given her to taste. The same with any reduced pâté, or sausage and cheeses recommended for quick sale. The small shopkeepers of the neighborhood, as avaricious as she was, were anxious to keep her miserable trade, and treated her with great respect. "Bonjour, madame," they would sing and point out the day's special, half-rotten bargain.

At one time, the architect and the underworld advocate and I were sitting in the small garden over the plans and we wanted to go to lunch. La mère machine came out protesting, wringing her hands and twisting her head left and right. Why waste money by going to a restaurant? She would serve luncheon in the garden—une blanquette de veau à l'ancienne. She must have found some ancient mushrooms under the stands that day, for she was not normally given to spending money for anything above wilted carrots, leeks and potatoes. She set the table and brought out wine. It was the only meal I ever ate in this house. It was very good and if I had left things as they were—the clochards in the

bistro, who brought a profit of $15 a day, la mère machine as the general factotum—everything would have been fine.

On a lovely morning, Jean came and with him a chef of the proper weight, face, voice and authority, beard and mustache. A good man. The chef sat down, and Jean spoke:

"Monsieur Tingaud is looking for you, as desperately as you are looking for him; he is of the grande cuisine; he will make your table famous. He is retired but the way things go in France, the uncertainty about the future . . . anyway, to make a long story short, we met, we talked and then I told him about the little palace here—La Colombe—and Monsieur Tingaud said, 'It sounds like exactly what I am looking for.'" The chef nodded and I told him how lucky that he had come before the final plans for the kitchen were drawn up; we could now benefit from his experience. The plans were inspected and some details changed; he found them in general very practical. The matter of salary was settled to mutual satisfaction. We drank a glass of Jupon and congratulated each other.

"I have never in my life seen anything like it," said Jean. "Everything falls into place as if by magic—the gods love you."

One day, Jean came and brought with him the head gardener of the Jardins du Luxembourg to look at our vine, or, as it is called in France, "the green tunnel." He pronounced the vine healthy and identified it as a Virginia creeper. He suggested that it be replanted in a new box, with earth which he would order. He had the box made, and the earth came, and two gardeners who replanted the vine and trimmed it. La mère machine looked at all this with suspicion and jabbered about the needless waste of money.

The two big gardeners not only were paid, but sat in the green tunnel after the work was done, and ate and drank, and the officials from the commissariat who had closed

an eye and accepted the uncertain date of my birth, and various other advisers and official personages also came, ate and drank. For the wine, which we had inherited from the former owner, la mère disappeared down the steps of a steep ladder into the cave, where she drew it from the barrel, and came up again to serve it. The business of the bar increased and we had steady income from the clochards, which la mère machine kept in a dreadful lead canister. This she shook with great energy and a bitter, contented smile when I came to the bistro toward evening.

After shaking the canister, she poked me with her outstretched index finger and said: "Leave this place as it is; listen to the advice of an old woman. This is a good affaire; you can live off it for the rest of your life."

Alas, I did not listen to her. The plans were going forward, and all that can go wrong with owning property, with building, with making alterations, with city ordinances, city architects, workmen and materials went wrong.

The dear little old house, the poetic corner, turned into a cathedral-sized nightmare. We had difficulties at every step with the government, with the Beaux Arts, with the architects of the city of Paris. With the prefecture of the police, the neighbors, the officials of the telephone monopoly, the water authority and most with the sewage authorities. When I speak of "we," I mean the clochard, the architect and I. What I attempted to do in a year takes in France normally five years of contemplation. There was never a "yes" or a "no," but grave doubting all along. All the people who had the power to make decisions warned us, with a finger to their noses, that all this would have to be carefully studied, weighed, passed on to others, considered, and was most probably in the end impossible.

One who has never filled out forms in France, who has never sat on a chair in a bureau of French officialdom has no idea of the might of functionaries. Nor of the time

45

they have on hand, of the many people who can lengthen this time and stretch it beyond the point where anything made of rubber, hemp or steel would snap. One problem, that of moving a stairway or a doorpost, can engage an entire floor of French bureaucrats for a month. In the case of Number 4 Rue de la Colombe, there was a magnificent opportunity for them to procrastinate, to detour, block and hamper, that could keep them busy until retirement, when fresh replacements would take over. Not only does the code, the law, the statute, ancient precedent and the opinion of the last judge enter into each minute decision; there is, moreover, the matter of the attitude of the officials on various levels toward you and your project, and the mood each one is in on a particular day. Does the official like you? Does he like your necktie, your nose? Does he feel that what you are doing is sensible? Will France be benefited by it? He will, as a judge and magistrate, examine you carefully; the lower his office the more weighty his manner. He will argue about the most abstract matter, the most remote, adverse possibilities of it. You will go through this rigmarole over and over again, and since I have no patience and am disinclined to humor defeatists and black-seers, we made snail's progress.

The patient architect, who sucked his cold pipe, wiped his glasses and his forehead and tried to establish a tolerable mood between the petitioner and the authority in a hundred offices. Eventually he said: "I think it is better I go alone, for this way we will never, never come to terms. You ask too much at once—an elevator, a roof garden, a cellar, a floor broken through, windows unbricked, gas, water, electricity. All this at once renders them dizzy. They detest you, in spite of my repeating every five minutes that you are 'un grand ami de la France,' and that your project will enhance the appearance of the Rue de la Colombe, and bring additional glory to Paris; they do not wish to see it in this light, at all. It is to them as if the money came out of their own pockets; it hurts them to see it so to say thrown away. You must not forget that to them the purchase of a pack of the cheapest cigarettes is a major decision. That you can, without reflection and concern, decide on all these things, and with impatience wave your hand over their objections, doesn't endear them to you. I must confess, dear friend, it sometimes upsets me too. I wish we had more time to sit and ponder this or that, but evidently yours is the American way of doing things, and I have been trying to adjust myself to it. I have had nightmares doing it. I dream of the skyline of New York and high buildings falling on me, and when I wake up I say to myself, 'Well, that's the way they do things in America. Evidently no one worries over there, especially not about money.' "

I was worried too, but I didn't want to upset the architect any more than he already was, and I suggested that from now on he go alone to deal with the officials.

Playwrights always have difficulties in eliminating a character when the person is no longer needed, and inventing a logical exit. But life itself is direct and brutally simple. One evening la mère machine went out; she had locked the bistro. In the Rue de la Colombe, fifty feet toward Notre Dame, an Arab hit her over the head and ran off with her purse, which contained the canister. She remembered all that in the Hôtel Dieu, the hospital which fortunately is right across the street, when she regained consciousness.

We took flowers to her and Jean sent her strong soup in bottles from the Méditerranée, and she lay in bed looking horrible, like a Buffet drawing, and with a Van Gogh kind of bandage around her head and her fists tightly balled. She reproached herself for the time she was wasting.

She replaced herself with two young girls, her nieces. They were of the group of sweet, underprivileged "little hands" that make up the largest body of the women of Paris. Of these, one who had no family was a part-time usher in a cinema and, unable to support herself that way, wanted to earn some extra money. The other came from a family where, with two little sisters, she had to share one bed. They owned one dress each and a pair of shoes. Both were eighteen.

"Get to work," commanded Jean.

He was a thorough man. He had had the stove going and on it a large pail with water, another waiting to be heated, and a third standing beside the girls, who had their sleeves rolled up and were scrubbing the floor of the dining room of the bistro. They emptied one pail in the street and a gray, greasy lukewarm soup ran down the gutter; a sick-making stench rose from it. The bistro stank awfully of the smells of sweat, of excrement, of unwashed people and of their filthy clothes. Bosie soaked up all the fleas in the house. The clochards, men and women, all drunk, stood around and gave me their dirty hands, paid in cash and left.

"They will never come back again—they are very polite people. They said good-by to you for good," remarked the professor.

"But why?"

"Because you're cleaning it up. That stench and stink of soap and hot water frightens them. Let's go out and get some fresh air—the dirt of centuries is being disturbed and it makes me ill."

The girls also came out for air. They looked awful, pale and thin, with dirty hands and arms, and they stank like the bistro. On the third day of cleaning, one of them said:

"You can't wash it off; it stays dirty. Everything is dirty. We have cleaned every day and washed the windows—there were windows suddenly where nobody thought there were windows. First we thought it was a board, then we washed and washed, and a gray light came in and a large rat jumped over the chair from a table. He must have eaten off the table and lived behind the closet."

They were rolling up their sleeves again.

"We excuse ourselves for speaking like this," said the one who had a family, sadly; and the other added cheerfully: "Oh, it will be better after today; it will be like living in the country."

"What makes you say that?"

D

"Oh, the beautiful green vine, the little garden. Excuse us, we must continue."

The house grew on me, in spite of all the difficulties or because of them. Although it was far from finished and I could not move into a room of it as yet, the joy of owning property covered me like a warm mantle. Even Bosie was delighted; at last he had a house to guard. I would meet the professor toward evening and we would walk across the Pont-Neuf, turn right at the statue of the Vert-galant, which is my favorite monument in Paris, and then walk along the Seine, through the flower market, finally coming to the house.

"The girls are right. Everything around here is like a dirty board; when you wash it long enough it becomes a window through which you see the past. As you know, I spend most of the cold days in the Louvre—it belongs to me now—and the very cold days I spend in the national archives, which are better heated. There is one good thing about the French, say what you please: they respect what they call your quality. When I pull out of your old suit the card which entitles me to entrance to various places, they are respectful, and when I sit down for my researches I am left undisturbed. Alors, here—I will explain to you why there is space in back of this house, and why this was called 'the street of hell.'

"There was a friseur and wigmaker shop here, where this garden is. It belonged to a man known in this neighborhood for his kindness and his devotion to Notre Dame. He shaved the priests and cut their tonsures. Back to back with the house that stood here, and facing Notre Dame, on the spot where you can park your car today, stood the house of his brother, who was a charcutier, famous for a marvelous pâté maison which the prelates of Notre Dame fancied, and which was exclusively sold to them. The priests lived in a row of houses close to the cathedral. The two houses of the brothers that stood here were linked by an underground passage. They prospered for many years, until by accident a dog digging for a bone led to the discovery of heinous crimes committed over a period of many years.

"You see, men wore wigs in those days and the friseur and wigmaker was in need of human hair. When someone, man or woman, with a likely head of hair entered his shop —and of course the best and loveliest hair was on the heads of the young—then, in the case of a man, he would start to shave him, after which he would cut his throat. In the case of a woman, he strangled her. The hair was then shorn off and used for wigs. The next step was to drag the body through the underground passage, over to the delicatessen shop, where the brother made it into sausages and famous pâté, so beloved by the priests of Notre Dame that there never was enough of it.

"When the dog had found the bone and the terrible butchery was discovered, the brothers were tried and executed—there across the river, in front of the Hôtel de Ville. They were torn into quarters by horses after torture. The houses were burned down. The Pope was in Avignon then, and a deputation of priests of Notre Dame went there, for, having eaten this unholy pâté for years, they felt impure and in need of special dispensation, which the Pope granted, with the proviso that no building should ever stand again where these two evil brothers had lived. In consequence of this, your little garden, your private square and your parking place. Alas, every foot of this ground is storied."

I proposed to the professor that he write a book about it.

"You write it," he said. "I will tell you all about the place, and you write it. But I thought you were going to paint, which I am afraid you never will, because something will always come in between, like this pâté." He looked strange for he had cut my overcoat off at an angle, which he said allowed him to walk more freely. He had done it simply with shears, clipping it like a hedge. The piece cut off had been made into a shawl and cap for the little girl.

The professor left. The girls were still scrubbing, and the place now smelled of insecticide and chlorine. The water was carried in a pitcher from a pump as it had been for hundreds of years. It was Sunday evening and I told them if they wanted to they could come to the Rue Gît-le-Coeur and take a bath. Afterward I would take them to dinner at the Méditerranée.

As we were eating, they explained: "We had no appetite at the Colombe—we could not even eat an apple there, it was so dirty." They drank some wine and then started to tell stories about the Colombe, about the architect and, with their hands held over their faces, about me, and what the neighbors said and thought. They laughed so hard that tears ran down their cheeks.

"Oh, it's wonderful," they said. "Like a theater—we learn so much—it has given us a new life—and freed us. We are like birds now. The wonderful people one meets— Claude Dauphin comes every day and has a glass of wine, and yesterday a Mister Buster Keaton was there and asked for you and he drank wine and gave each of us a thousand francs. Last week we divided sixteen thousand francs between ourselves. Such good fortune doesn't come to everyone. We are so grateful."

I then had to go to New York but rushed back as soon as I could with the impatience that is part of my make-up. I had announced the opening of the house—much too soon. Not even the rooms were done. The architect had become imaginative and had got students of the Beaux Arts to come one week end to paint the two lower floors. I painted décor on the wet walls. More students got the rest of the house in order. Music and food were arranged for. The housewarming was imminent.

At this point Jean appeared and with him the chef, Monsieur Tingaud. "Don't let what this one has to say upset you," started Jean unhappily, raising his hands. "Quelle catastrophe!" he wailed, looking with disgust at the chef.

The chef broke in: "I hope monsieur will understand. First of all I must say that I regret the matter, that is, I am in a way sorry. For I am certain that I would have been happy here, and that we would have understood each other. But I cannot come and cook here. Why not? Because, monsieur, I cannot afford it. Do you understand?"

"Please come to the point, monsieur," said Jean.

"The world is vastly changing and everything with it," he went on.

Jean became impatient. "We know, we know. Tell what has happened."

"One day I was walking down the Rue du Bac," started the chef, but Jean let out a moan and ran his fingers through his hair and said: "He has taken a job in a factory, can you understand that?"

The chef was now in a temper and, pushing Jean aside, said: "I have been offered the position of executive director of the kitchens of the Renault factory."

Jean put his fists on his hips and said: "He is in charge of a mess hall for mechanics; he has folie de grandeur."

The chef answered: "Perhaps, perhaps, but neither of you could afford to pay my salary—and the conditions, the conditions—you could not offer me those in a thousand years." He held up one finger and pointed: "One meal a day, one dish to cook. I come to work at nine, I go home at five. Two weeks' holiday with pay. Pension, medical and dental and other benefits. My kitchen of ten electric stoves looks very much like an operating room."

Jean shook his head: "And you are proud of this? Tell me how many of this one dish you serve a day?"

"Seven thousand and some hundreds."

"Well, bon appétit, monsieur."

"I am sorry, I did not mean to brag," said the chef.

"Oh, don't be sorry," said Jean. "There are still cooks in France with some pride!"

Now they came close to each other and the chef yelled: "Pride for what? Pride to stand fourteen hours behind a stove, pride for being underpaid, and to cook a hundred things and listen to complaints and to have a miserable proprietor watch every gram of butter and cry in your ear? No thank you." Without saying good-by and in haste, Monsieur Tingaud stalked off in the direction of Notre Dame.

"Don't worry," said Jean to me. "We are going to save ourselves. I will cook myself if all else fails." He left muttering.

I had invited for the housewarming about fifty people, who had accepted, when the architect with pipe in hand came running and informed me that it would be impossible to give the party, because we would have no toilet.

"The final permission has not been granted," he said sadly. "It will not be ready."

In agony of mind I wrote a letter to Air France, to TWA, to BOAC and Pan-Am, asking if they would lend us mobile equipment necessary for the comfort of guests. Air France as well as all the other airlines sent their regrets; it was the height of the tourist season and they were in need of all their ambulatory conveniences.

I finally settled the matter by buying an old taxi. On the right door I had neatly lettered MESSIEURS and on the left MESDAMES and made an arrangement with Jean, so that the taxi would go back and forth from my place to the Méditerranée whenever the need arose.

The party was a great success. I said to the architect as I left for America again the next day, "Finish the bathrooms first, no matter what it costs. I give you carte blanche." He brought a paper to the plane at Orly Airport, which I shall forever be sorry I signed. The house had by now eaten immense sums. I had to go back to America and do some work quickly to earn more money.

When I returned, I rushed to the house to see how far things had progressed. It was toward evening, the lamps were lit, and in back of my house stood Notre Dame, floodlit. The effect was grandiose and exciting, and as I surveyed the scene I was glad that I had done it all. It was perfect. As I went down the short way to the small square where the house stood, I saw that there was a large hill inside the garden. It was of earth. Children were playing on top of it. Through a large hole in the street I saw a man below filling the stuff into sacks with a shovel; about a hundred such sacks were neatly tied

and stacked on the steps against the side of the house to the right of mine. The street was barred and a red lantern hung on the barrier. I asked the man what he was doing. "An American millionaire is putting bathrooms into this house," he said and kept on shoveling. A truck came and loaded the sacks and took them away.

At the time I had bought the house, some forty people lived in it and all shared one toilet, consisting of a large square stone with a hole in its center. It stood in a recess under the circular stone stairs. A door of a few painted planks nailed together, hung on iron hinges, gave it privacy. The stone was a historic memento, having been visited by François Villon, François Premier and La belle Ferronnière. The venerable black stone stood under the special protection of the Beaux Arts and nobody could move it.

But, because I was "un grand ami de la France," the august body charged with the care of national monuments extended me their tolerance to the extent that I was allowed to install sanitary facilities elsewhere in the building.

When this work began in my absence, the worst happened. It was discovered that the sewers of Paris were some two hundred yards away from the Rue de la Colombe. It was also discovered that the foundation of Number 4 was the same as that on which Notre Dame stands, the Roman wall of the ancient Lutetia. If a pneumatic drill were used, the disturbance caused would, like an earth tremor, carry from boulder to boulder to the Cathedral, and saints, stone ornaments or gargoyles might fall off the edifice. Therefore, it was necessary to do this work by hand. All day there were two men with an acetylene lamp, busy carefully chipping through the ancient stone and tunneling toward the sewers of Paris. The underworld lawyer calculated that each sack of debris cost me a hundred dollars. He had so far counted 260 sacks.

The next day, the clochard stood in horror, fascinated, when he saw me. I had lost some ten pounds. He also had changed. It was getting cold, he had stopped shaving and grown a beard. He was wearing the blue coat and the bowler; the little girl held his hand.

La Belle Ferronière

"I am sorry I had anything to do with this," he said, pointing with his cane at the house, the sacks of white dust and chips of the Roman wall.

I reflected, which I rarely do, and always too late. The clochard said: "Take my advice, turn your back on it. Do the way I did and throw everything out of the window. If you don't, this house will eat you. You will never be through with its difficulties. This is a cursed and haunted building and it doesn't want anyone to touch it." I followed his advice.

Bosie performs for me the functions of the picture of Dorian Grey. When we left, when I had gotten rid of the old house, he looked as awful as I felt inside.

CLOCHARDS, PARIS
Gouache, 1958.   22″ x 27½″

3.

A PLACE TO PAINT

Halfway between Paris and Versailles, on the side road that leads across the park of St. Cloud, is a place called Ville-d'Avray. There, several hundred years old, facing the lake of Corot, stands an old tavern, called the Hostellerie Cabassud. I had stopped there for years. It is a quaint place, with good kitchen and cellar; part of it is a small hotel in which one can rent rooms overlooking the lake, for a very reasonable price. There are old chestnut trees; the restaurant part of the hotel consists of little huts, as in *Robinson Crusoe*, built up into the trees.

Searching for places to paint, I wandered through the streets and the gardens of the Hostellerie itself. On the grounds I found hidden behind trees and covered with vines a high square pavillon, a glasshouse almost, which was used to store old furniture. The proprietor of the place told me that it had been built long ago as a ballroom for dances and the celebrations of local societies, like the volunteer firemen, but that it had not been used for the last eighty years.

He was agreeable to have it cleared and cleaned and it became my studio. I paint there now, and every morning walk around the lake of Corot. Silent fishermen sit there. An old weeping willow washes her hair in the waters, all is of muted color. It is like Gmunden, with swans and waterfall, humid, and one can drink the air rather than breathe it. There is a corner of this lake where the words from the *Tempest* always echo: "Ye elves of hills, brooks, standing lakes, and groves."

The groves are there, the hills, the brook, the standing lakes, and water gurgles from one down to the other, and eventually to the hidden summerhouse where Corot painted. To this a bridge leads, covered with moss, water grasses and bluebells. The trunks of trees are of dark green hue.

In the years there, I painted some of the nearby scenery, also Paris, people, greenhouses and sheltered little retreats.

And I started to paint in oil, from which I had always shied away, having persuaded myself that I could not stand the smell or feel of oil and turpentine; also that I could not wait for oil to dry. The last excuse was valid. For while I look at an object for a long time, and make many sketches and go back and look again and again, when finally I paint it is done in a kind of urgent fury. It goes quickly or not at all.

Everything in this life has its consequences, and unfortunate happenings hold compensations. At the Colombe, under the greenery of the Virginia creeper, I had met a painter, by name Marcel Salinas. Salinas is not only an artist of independence, individual

style and talent, he is also a savant, who knows the ancient techniques and has invented new ones. He makes his own India inks because the ones he finds in shops are not intense enough for him. As intense as his ink are his eyes and his spirit. He does a kind of sorcerer's cuisine with his thin fingers, using ancient formulas, and during this process a constant recitation goes on which covers the whole history of art from the caveman to the present. I've begged him to have this recorded.

I helped Salinas put on an exhibition in New York. In return he said he would help me to get over my reluctance to use oils. We sat and talked in Paris and in New York. He came to my studio with various little bottles, among them one with a mixture called *siccatif*. He talked to me as one does to a horse about to bolt and run, to whose halter one holds on.

"I know you don't like to hear this—you don't want to listen." He arranged his bottles. "It is very simple; I know you are not listening to a word I say to you, but just the same, just look how I do it, it is childishly easy, it won't hurt. Now just watch

me, a tiny little bit of this and a little bit of that—and always use Mars black. Mars black you cannot get in Europe, so take it with you. A tube will suffice. Other blacks don't dry, and beware of Prussian blue—that takes an eternity—here is a green which you would never think you could obtain. Watch me."

He mixed tiny smears of color and there was a very intense black green, darker than vert anglais—the precise color I had wanted for the tree trunks in Corot's garden.

"Ah, you see now you are interested. Now just a little on this small brush. Now take it to the canvas and now paint. Make a line—there—it's easy—that is all there is—the rest you know already because you always painted as with oils, only you did it with gouache. Now try to copy yourself in oils. Here is a picture."

He took a small brush, squeezed a tiny drop of paint on a newspaper—which is a good palette, for it absorbs oily substances—mixed color with it, and handed me the brush. I had a picture of the harbor of Les Sables-d'Olonne in front of me, which I had painted in gouache, and he asked me to copy the picture. To my great surprise, at once and without smelling badly, or at least no longer offending me, the picture was there in oil. This was a moment of great liberation.

Salinas, in repose, looks like an El Greco monk doing penance. In moments of ecstasy he glows in a green light like Lazarus being raised from the dead. He said in this last mood: "Voilà, you have it, that is all I can tell you. That is the complete lesson. Now let yourself go." He promised to come back the next day.

I bought a large canvas and the supplies necessary for making this new kind of cuisine. In the car I had a five-gallon gas can and in this I mixed the solution and shook it. Salinas came in as I was about to apply it to the canvas. He looked and said: "What's this in the jerrycan?"

I told him it was the solution. I also had a plain flat housepainter's brush. He said: "You want to paint your room in oil?"

I said: "No no, I am starting on a picture." He ran out without a word, and I did not see him again for months.

For two months I destroyed everything I painted in oil. I suffered the peculiar agonies of a painter's hell—the inability to carry the picture that you have in mind to the canvas.

I burned about thirty more in the studio in Ville-d'Avray, and for a while went back to gouache. Then one day, I came out of the morass, the nightmarish uncertainty lifted like the heavy fog from the lake and the canvas brightened.

It was a happy time, with all my energy engaged, and all outside the subject of the picture of no concern. If painting goes well, then it goes that way like a happy little train running through a landscape, whistling. And the picture is there forever; it looks back at you, and thanks you. It has its own clear voice and says it day and night and forever.

*On the following pages are the gouaches and oils
done in the period from 1954 to 1958.*

RUE COROT. VILLE D'AVRAY
Oil, 1957.   25½" x 32"

FISHING BOAT, HONFLEUR
Oil, 1958.   23½″ x 32″

57

COUPLE EATING ÉCREVISSES, MAXIM'S, PARIS
Oil, 1958. 36″ x 26″

GARDEN HOUSE, VILLE D'AVRAY
Oil, 1957.   15″ x 22″

PORTRAIT IN YELLOW. VILLE D'AVRAY
Oil, 1957.   22″ x 18″

CHURCH OF PLAISIR. SEINE-ET-OISE
Oil, 1957.   58″ x 45½″

WOMAN AND DOG, RÔTISSERIE PÉRIGOURDINE
Gouache, Paris, 1955.   24½″ x 17½″

RESTAURANT BOATS ON THE SEINE
Oil, 1957.   26″ x 36½″

GARDEN HOUSE OF COROT. VILLE D'AVRAY
Oil, 1957. 26″ x 36½″

HONFLEUR. THE INNER BASIN
Oil, 1957.   23½″ x 32″

THE SEINE AT ST. CLOUD
Oil, 1957. 32″ x 39½″

GYPSY CHILDREN BATHING, MARLY-LE-ROI
Oil, 1957.   26″ x 36″

ALLÉE DE LA FÉLICITÉ. PARC DE ST. CLOUD
Oil, 1957.   36″ x 28½″

SWANS AND CHESTNUT TREES. VILLE D'AVRAY
Oil, 1957.   25″ x 36″

HOTHOUSE WITH YELLOW FLOWERS, BOUGIVAL
Oil, 1957.   57½" x 45"

HONFLEUR, LOW TIDE
Oil, 1957.   23½″ x 32″

RED-HAIRED WOMAN AND DOG. VILLE D'AVRAY
Oil, 1957.   36" x 26"

NUNS RETURNING FROM MARKET. LES HALLES, PARIS
Oil, 1957.   26″ x 36″

ALBI
Oil, 1957.   58″ x 45½″

SQUARE AND CHURCH, MARLY-LE-ROI
Oil, 1957.   26″ x 36″

"LE VERT-GALANT" SEEN FROM BELOW. PARIS
Oil, 1957.   58" x 45½"

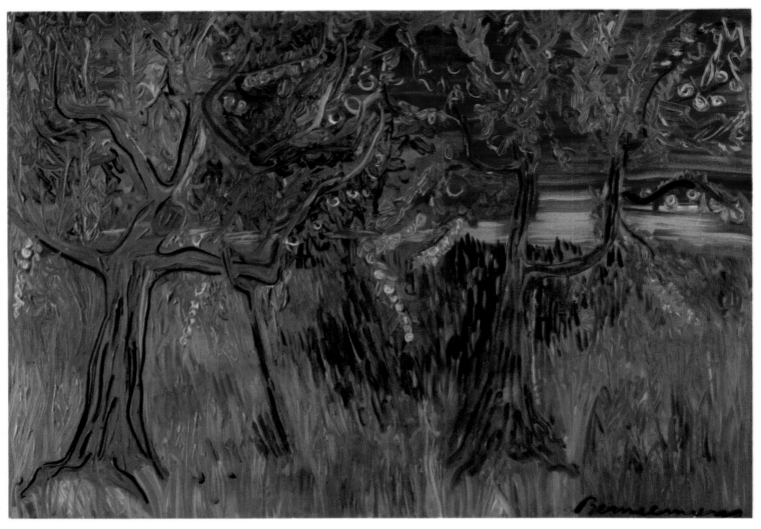

SUNSET, HONFLEUR
Oil, 1957.   26″ x 36″

STATUE OF "LE VERT-GALANT" WITH RED HOUSES, PARIS
Oil, 1957.   32″ x 23½″

LE PONT-NEUF. PARIS
Oil, 1957.   26″ x 36″

LAKE IN SPRING. VILLE D'AVRAY
Oil, 1957.   25½" x 32"

DODO D'HAMBOURG. CRAZY HORSE SALOON. PARIS
Oil, 1957.   58″ x 45″

PONT DES ARTS AND INSTITUT DE FRANCE. PARIS
Oil, 1957.   45″ x 58″

CLOCHARDS UNDER THE PONT-NEUF. PARIS
Oil, 1957.   23½″ x 32″